BALLPOINT BANANAS
AND OTHER JOKES FOR KIDS

By Charles Keller
Illustrated by David Barrios

Prentice-Hall, Inc., Englewood Cliffs, N.J.

For Coby, Bayard, Paul and Jacqueline

Printed in the United States of America   2

Prentice-Hall International, Inc., London
Prentice-Hall of Australia, Pty. Ltd., North Sydney
Prentice-Hall of Canada, Ltd., Toronto
Prentice-Hall of India Private Ltd., New Delhi
Prentice-Hall of Japan, Inc., Tokyo

Library of Congress Cataloging in Publication Data

Keller, Charles, comp.
  Ballpoint bananas and other jokes for kids.

  SUMMARY: A selection of riddles and humorous
rhymes, both traditional and contemporary.
  Bibliography: p.
  1. Wit and humor, Juvenile. [1. Joke books.
2. Riddles. 3. Humorous poetry] I. Barrios,
David, illus. II. Title.
PZ8.7.K42Bal   398.6   72-7338
ISBN 0-13-055350-6

Contents

RIDDLES

5

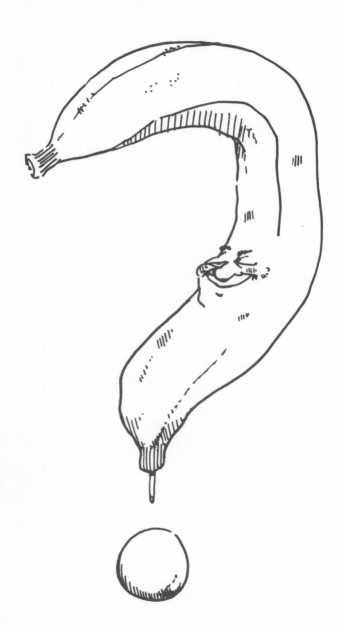

6

Fruit Salad

What is yellow and goes click-click?

Why were the little strawberries upset?

How do you make a pumpkin squash?

A ball-point banana.

Because their mother and father were in a jam.

Throw it up in the air and it comes down squash.

8

What is red and goes slam-slam-slam-slam?

What's purple, weighs 2 tons and lives at the bottom of the sea?

A four-door apple.

Moby Grape.

Animal Crackers

Why is a rabbit's nose so shiny?

11

His powder puff is on the wrong end.

What is gray, has four legs and a trunk?

What is even more remarkable than a horse that can count?

What do you get when you cross an octopus with a bale of hay?

What is green and slimy, lives in swamps and ponds, and is quite dangerous?

13

A mouse going on a long vacation.

A spelling bee.

Eight straw brooms.

A frog with a hand grenade.

Here Come The Elephants!

Why do elephants have wrinkled legs?

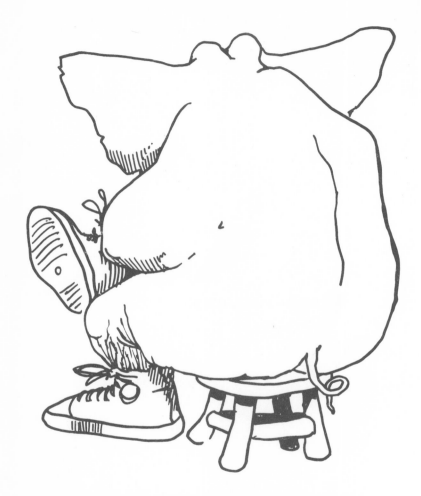

From tying their tennis shoes too tight.

16

Why do elephants wear trunks?

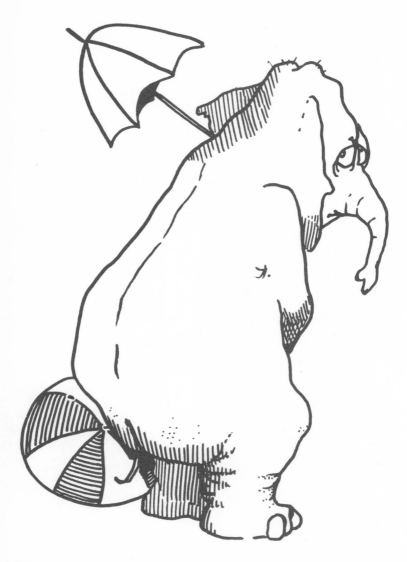

So they won't be embarrassed when they go
swimming.

18

How can you tell if there is an elephant in your refrigerator?

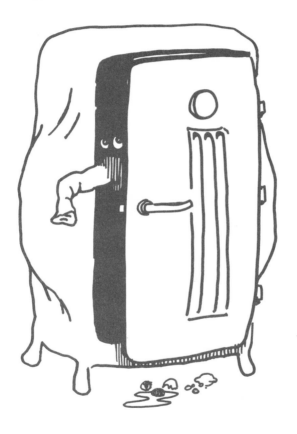

How can you prevent an elephant from charging?

Why do elephants have pointed tails?

19

By the footprints in the jello.

Take away his credit card.

From standing too close to the pencil sharpener.

20

How do you make an elephant float?

What is red and white on the outside and gray on the inside?

How do you make an elephant light?

Two scoops of ice cream, some root beer and one elephant.

Campbell's Cream of Elephant soup.

Stick his tail in the socket.

22

Why did the elephant sit on the marshmallow?

What is the difference between an elephant and a peanut-butter sandwich?

23

To keep from falling in the hot chocolate.

An elephant doesn't stick to the roof of your mouth.

History's Mysteries

Why was George Washington buried standing up?

Because he never lied.

26

Why is it useless to send a telegram to Washington?

If the green house is on the left side of the road and the red house is on the right side of the road, where is the white house?

What did Paul Revere say when he finished his famous ride?

If April showers bring May flowers, what do May flowers bring?

What was Ben Franklin's kite made of?

Because he's dead.

In Washington.

Whoa.

Pilgrims.

Fly paper.

Chilling Chuckles

What color is a ghost?

Boo.

What kind of monster do you find in a wash-
ing machine?

31

A wash-and-wear wolf.

How does a monster count up to fifteen?

Where does a witch keep her space ship?

Why did King Kong climb the Empire State Building?

33

On his fingers.

In her broom closet.

To get his kite back.

34

What do you do with a blue monster?

35

Cheer him up.

What Did He Say?

What did the monkey say when his sister had a baby?

37

I'll be a monkey's uncle.

What did the ocean say when the plane flew over it?

What did the polluted water say to the filter?

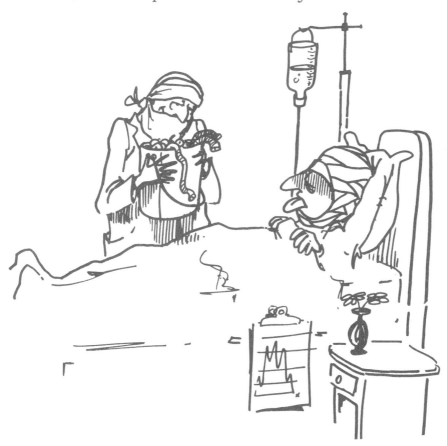

What did the doctor say to the patient after he finished the operation?

Nothing. It just waved.

I hope I make myself clear.

That will be enough out of you.

40

What did the nail say to the hammer?

41

Why don't you hit someone your own size?

42

Mind Benders

What do you do if your toe falls off?

Call a tow truck.

44

Why is a doctor the stingiest man on earth?

45

Because he treats you and then makes you pay
for it.

How do locomotives hear?

Why is your nose in the middle of your face?

47

Through their engineers.

Because it's the scenter.

48

If an athlete gets athlete's foot, what does an astronaut get?

49

Missile toe.

For The Birds

Why do hummingbirds hum?

51

Because they don't know the words.

52

Where do baby elephants come from?

What would you have if a bird got caught in your lawn mower?

What does a 500 pound canary say?

53

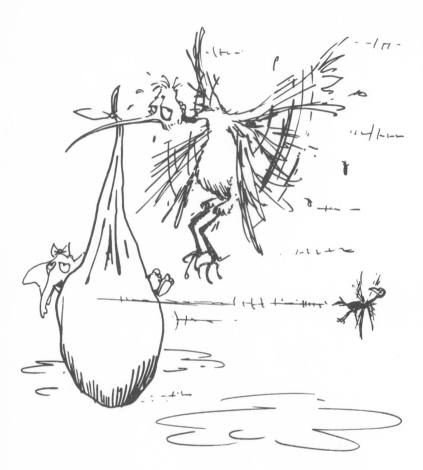

Great big storks.

Shredded tweet.

Here kitty, kitty.

54

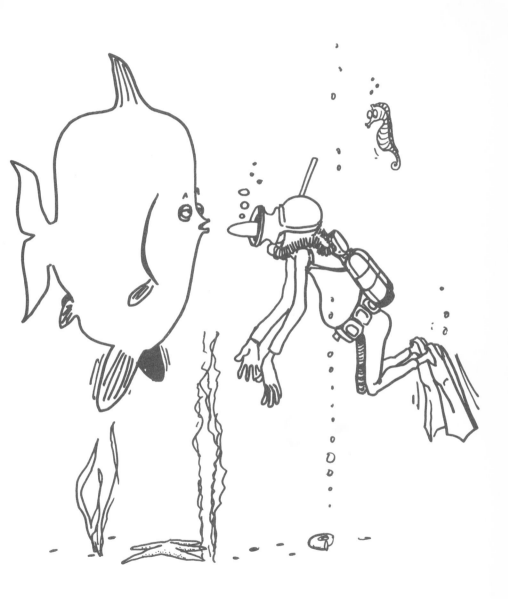

What do you call a frightened skin diver?

55

Chicken of the sea.

RHYMES

57

58

Kiss Me Quick

You love yourself, you think you're grand,
You go to the movies and hold your hand.
You put your arms around your waist,
And when you get fresh you slap your face.

A kiss is a germ or so it's been stated,
But kiss me quick, I've been vaccinated.

60

I love you, I love you,
I love you, I do,
But don't get excited,
I love monkeys too.

I wish I was a china cup
From which you drank your tea,
And every time you took a sip,
You'd give a kiss to me.

Take My Advice

Tobacco is a nasty weed;
It's the devil that sows the seed;
It soils your pockets, scents your clothes
And makes a chimney of your nose.

When boating never quarrel
For you will find, no doubt,
A boat is not the proper place
To have a falling out.

Dr. Brown fell in the well
And broke his collarbone.
Why didn't he cure the sick
And leave the well alone?

I like coffee, I like tea
I like the boys and the boys like me.
Tell your mother to hold her tongue
For she did the same when she was young.
Tell your father to do the same,
For he was the one who changed her name.

A fool will never change his mind
And who can think it strange?
The reason's clear, for fools, my friend,
Have no mind to change.

65

An apple a day keeps the doctor away.
An onion a day
Keeps everyone away.

Cat Tales

Linda had a little cat,
She fed it on tin cans;
And when the cat had kittens
They came in Ford sedans.

There once were two cats from Kilkenny,
Each thought there was one cat too many;
So they quarreled and fit,
They scratched and they bit,
Then, instead of two cats, there weren't any.

There's music in a hammer,
There's music in a nail,
There's music in a pussycat
When you step upon its tail.

Tales That Grow Out Of My Head

Algy met a bear.
The bear was bulgy.
The bulge was Algy.

Sitting on a tombstone
A ghost came up and said,
"I'm sorry to disturb you
But you're sitting on my head."

70

I went to the river, and I couldn't get across.
I jumped on an alligator, thought it was a horse.
I spurred him with my heels, and he began to roar.
I nearly burned the water up a-getting to the shore.

72

Twisted Tales

A maid with a duster made a furious bluster
Dusting a bust in the hall.
When the bust, it was dusted,
The bust, it was busted,
The bust, it was dust.
That is all!

Mr. See and Mr. Soar were old friends. See owned a saw and Soar owned a seesaw. Now See's saw sawed Soar's seesaw before Soar saw See, which made Soar sore. Had Soar seen See's saw before See saw Soar's seesaw, then See's saw would not have sawed Soar's seesaw. But See saw Soar's seesaw before Soar saw See's saw so See's saw sawed Soar's seesaw. It was a shame to let See see Soar so sore because See's saw sawed Soar's seesaw.

Forget Me Not

Remember Grant
Remember Lee
The heck with them
Remember me.

Forget me not,
For if you do
You'll feel the weight
Of my big shoe.

75

Remember me when far away
And only half awake.
Remember me on your wedding day
And send to me some cake.

Tell me quick
Before I faint,
Is we friends
Or is we ain't?

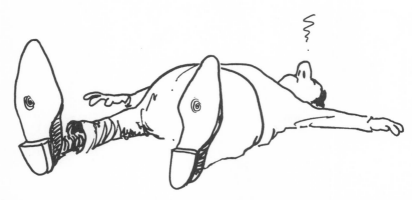

School Daze

Now I lay me down to rest,
I pray to pass tomorrow's test;
If I should die before I wake,
That's one less test I'll have to take.

God made the bees,
The bees make honey;
We do the work
And teacher makes the money.

Birds on the mountain,
Fish in the sea;
How you ever passed
Is a mystery to me.

An eagle flew from North to South
And caught our teacher in the mouth.
When he saw she was a fool
He dropped her here to teach our school.

Roses are red,
Violets are blue,
I copied your paper
And I flunked too.

Mixed-Up
Mother Goose

Little Jack Horner sat in a corner,
Watching the girls go by.
Along came a beauty; he said, "Hello Cutie"
And that's how he got his black eye.

79

Mary had a little lamb,
A little pork, a little jam
A little fish, a little ham
A little soda topped with fizz;
Now how sick our Mary is.

There was an old man who had a wooden leg.
He wouldn't steal and he wouldn't beg;
He took four spools and an old tin can
He called it a Ford, and the darn thing ran.

80

Animal Fare

A centipede was happy quite
Until a frog in fun
Said, "Pray, which leg comes after which?"
This raised her mind to such a pitch
She lay distracted in the ditch,
Considering how to run.

I had a little pig and his name was Ben,
He learned to count from one to ten;
I dressed him up to look like a clerk
With a collar and tie and sent him to work.

My dog Rover is a clever little pup—
He stands upon his hind legs
When you hold his front ones up.

There was a little boy and he had a little dog,
And he taught that dog to beg.
And that dear little dog at dinner time
Would stand upon one leg.
One day to his master's surprise
That doggy said, "Here goes!"
And he cocked his hind legs in the air
And stood upon his nose.

LAUGHING STOCK

85

86

Taunts and Teases

Ask me no questions,
Tell you no lies;
Keep your mouth shut
And you'll catch no flies.

Minnie's got a feller,
Ten feet tall,
Sleeps in the kitchen,
With his feet in the hall.

Fatty on a broomstick.
Fatty in the sea.
Fatty got stung
By a bumblebee.

Lincoln, Lincoln I've been thinking,
What in the world have you been drinking?
Smells like whiskey, tastes like wine,
Oh my gosh! It's turpentine!

Made you look, made you stare,
Made the barber cut your hair.
Cut it long, cut it short,
Cut it with a knife and fork.

Just because you smell, don't think you're a big cheese.
Just because you have a pointed head, don't think you're sharp.

Hay is for horses,
Straw is for cows,
Milk is for babies
For crying out loud.

89

God made the French.
God made the Dutch.
Whoever made you
Didn't make much.

Skinny, Skinny, took a bath,
Didn't tell a soul.
Forgot to put the plunger in,
And fell right down the hole.

Who's That Knocking At My Door?

Knock, knock.
Who's there?
Oswald.
Oswald who?
Oswald my gum.

Knock, knock.
Who's there?
Chesterfield.
Chesterfield who?
Chesterfield my leg
 so I slapped him.

Knock, knock.
Who's there?
The Avon lady,
Your doorbell's broken.

Knock, knock.
Who's there?
Wendy.
Wendy who?
Wendy joke is finished, you'd better laugh.

Knock, knock.
Who's there?
Butch, Jimmy and Joe
Butch, Jimmy and Joe who?
Butch your arms around me, Jimmy a kiss,
or I'll Joe home.

Ask Me No Questions

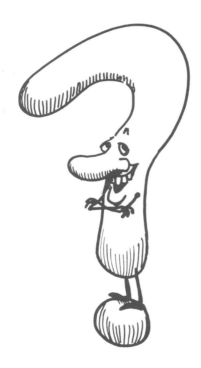

What's your name?
Pudding Tame. Ask me again I'll tell you the same.
Buster Brown. Ask me again I'll knock you down.
Pudding Pie. Ask me again and I'll make you cry.
President Monroe. Ask me again, you still won't know.

What time is it?
Daytime going on nighttime.
Time all the monkeys' tails fell off. Isn't yours loose?
Time you bought a watch.
A freckle past a hair.

Do you like butter?
I'll push you in the gutter.
Do you like jelly?
I'll punch you in the belly.
Do you like pie?
I'll hit you in the eye.
Do you want a nickel?
Go suck on a pickle.

94

Look up.
Look down.
See my thumb?
Gee you're dumb.
See my feet?
You're so neat!
See my hair?
You're a square!
See my nose?
You need new clothes!

Suggestions for Further Reading

———. *Little Joke Book*. New York, Peter Pauper Press, 1962.

Bruce, Dana. *Tell Me A Joke*. New York, Platt, 1966.

Cerf, Bennett. *Bennett Cerf's Houseful of Laughter*. New York, Random, 1963.

Charlip, Remy. *Arm in Arm*. New York, Parents, 1970.

Clarke, David. *Jokes, Puns and Riddles*. New York, Doubleday, 1969.

Emrich, Duncan. *The Nonsense Book*. New York, Four Winds, 1970.

Longman, Harold. *Would You Put Your Money in a Sandbank?*, New York, Rand, 1969.

Hoke, Helen. *Jokes, Jokes, Jokes*. New York, Watts, 1963.

———. *More Jokes, Jokes, Jokes*. New York, Watts, 1965.

Wood, Ray. *Fun in American Folk Rhymes*. Lippincott, 1952.

398.6   13401
K
Keller, Charles
Ballpoint bananas and other
jokes for kids

DATE DUE			
APR 2 1 1978			
FEB 6 1980			
MAR 4 1980			
JUN 8 198?			
MAY 0 5 199?			